THE
SAN FRANCISCO
WATERFRONT
COOKBOOK

THE
SAN FRANCISCO
WATERFRONT
COOKBOOK

Joseph Orlando

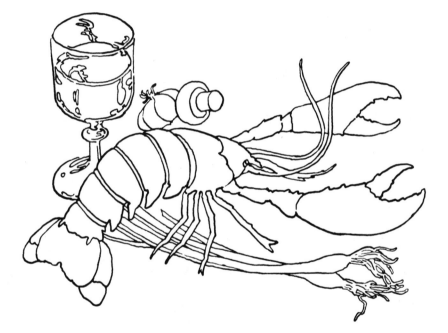

CELESTIALARTS
Berkeley, California

Cover:
Golden Gate Bridge and San Francisco skyline.
Photo © Ted Streshinsky/Photo 20–20

Illustrations: Tom Cervenak

Revised Edition

Cover and text design by David Charlsen
Composition by Recorder Typesetting Network

Library of Congress Catalog Card Number 91-91864
ISBN 0–89087–652–5

FIRST PRINTING 1991
5   4   3   2   1
95   94   93   92   91

Printed in the United States of America

Contents

Foreword

In prehistoric times, one of the ancestors of the human race discovered a piece of meat that had been exposed to flame. He or she tasted it and decided it was a marked improvement over the raw diet of the time. From such a random experience, the art of cooking was probably born. Since that happy day, people have continually searched for new and different ways to prepare food. The preparation of food has become a hobby for some, a livelihood for others, and a source of enjoyment for all. My hope is that the recipes in this book will tantalize your taste buds and bring you pleasure.

My forebears came from the craggy hills and sun-washed beaches of Sicily, an isolated island where food staples were limited but fish were abundant. This heritage set the stage for developing Italian cooking to a fine art in San Francisco where the abundance of seafood, spices, and other ingredients in this port city allowed full rein to the talents of Italian chefs. San Francisco is known the world over as a mecca for food lovers.

In this guide to good meals, we have collected recipes that have stood the test of time from the bleak landscape of Sicily to the blue waters of San Francisco Bay, always keeping in mind that gourmet cooking and eating may be enjoyed by all. These recipes will provide tantalizing taste experiences.

Bon Appétit!

Joseph J. Orlando

Alioto's No. 8

Fisherman's Wharf
San Francisco

Sautéed Lobster Tails

Clean and peel six lobster tails. Sauté in garlic butter 6 to 8 minutes. Transfer to heated platter.

Heat a serving of cooked rice in the pan in which lobster was sautéed. Place in serving dish and arrange lobster tails on top. Cover with **Mustard Sauce** (see recipe below) and glaze under a broiler.

Serves three.

Mustard Sauce

1 cup Cream Sauce
1 tablespoon (prepared) mustard
1 teaspoon cold water

Mix mustard with water. Stir mixture into **Cream Sauce** (see page 101) about 2 minutes before serving. The quantity of mustard may be increased or decreased to make the flavor strong or mild as desired.

Makes 1 cup.

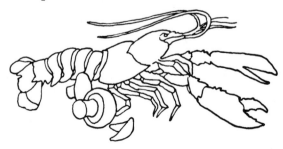

Crab Mornay en Casserole

2 cups rich Cream Sauce
2 teaspoons sherry wine
2 cups fresh cooked crabmeat
4 slices American cheese
Paprika, as desired
Melted butter, as required

Into each of four individual casseroles pour ½ cup **Cream Sauce** (see page 101), to which wine has been added. Add layer of ½ cup crabmeat, and top with a slice of cheese. Sprinkle each casserole with paprika and butter.

Bake in moderate oven (350 degrees) for 10 minutes, and serve hot.

Serves four.

N. Alioto's Captain's Cabin Restaurant

155 Jefferson
Fisherman's Wharf
San Francisco

Crab Legs Sauté

Dust one pound of crab legs in flour, and sauté quickly in 4 tablespoons of butter. Add sliced mushrooms and chopped green onions. Add a small amount of chopped canned tomatoes, salt, pepper, sauterne wine. Simmer for 5 minutes.

Serve on a bed of rice.

Serves four.

Frankie's Special Salad

This excellent recipe came from my mother, who made it on special days.

To one pound of crab or baby shrimp in a large bowl, add celery hearts, cut on a slant. Add one avocado, cut into slices. Season to taste with salt and pepper. Add olive oil and vinegar. Toss, and allow to stand in the refrigerator for at least 2 hours. Serve on lettuce, with a sliced tomato.

Serves four.

Borruso's Lighthouse Seafood Grotto

Fisherman's Wharf
San Francisco

Sauce à la Creole

2 cups onions, sliced julienne style
2 cups celery, sliced julienne style
3 tablespoons butter
2 cups tomato sauce
2 cups tomato purée or tomato paste
2 cups bell peppers, sliced julienne style
1 clove garlic, finely chopped
3 whole bay leaves
1 tablespoon oregano
1 tablespoon monosodium glutamate
1 teaspoon thyme
1 teaspoon salt
1 teaspoon pepper
2 cups beef stock or water

Braise onions and celery until half cooked in butter. Add tomato sauce, purée, peppers, garlic, bay leaves, oregano, monosodium glutamate, thyme, salt, and pepper. Simmer for 3 minutes, and add beef stock or water. Simmer for 2 hours, stirring frequently to keep sauce from sticking to bottom of pot.

Makes 1½ quarts.

Lobster Thermidor

1 pound lobster, diced
3 tablespoons butter
1 cup sliced mushrooms, canned or fresh
1 cup chopped onion or shallots
1 clove garlic, finely chopped
2 tablespoons chopped pimentos
1 tablespoon chopped parsley
½ teaspoon oregano
½ teaspoon monosodium glutamate
Salt and pepper to taste
½ cup sherry wine
Newburg Sauce
Grated Parmesan cheese

Sauté lobster in butter in a heavy saucepan. Add mushrooms, onions, garlic, pimentos, parsley, oregano, monosodium glutamate, salt and pepper, and wine. Cook for 2 minutes. Add **Newburg Sauce** (see recipe below).

Place mixture in lobster shells. Cover with grated Parmesan cheese or **Hollandaise Sauce** (see page 101), and bake for 15 to 20 minutes in 400-degree oven.

Serves two.

Newburg Sauce

Make a thick **Cream Sauce** (see page 101). Add coloring to acquire desired egg shade. Add wine to taste.

Caesar's Restaurant

2299 Powell Street
San Francisco

Julius Caesar's Favorite Dessert Zabaione à la Caesar's

5 egg yolks, plus 1 whole egg
3 tablespoons sugar
½ cup Marsala or rum
A dash of vanilla
A dash of egg coloring

Combine egg yolks, egg and sugar. Pour into double-boiler above simmering water, or a medium size heat-proof glass bowl set in a shallow pan of barely simmering water.

Beat mixture with wire whisk or rotary beater until it is pale yellow and fluffy. Gradually add marsala or rum and continue beating until the zabaione is thick enough to hold its shape. This may take as long as ten minutes. Spoon out the zabaione into individual dessert glasses, bowls or compotes. Serve while still hot, or it may be served chilled. Decorate with whipped cream.

Chicken Cacciatore

2 whole chickens (2 lbs. each)
2 cups flour
¼ cup olive oil
2 tablespoons butter
1 pound fresh mushrooms, sliced, or 1 cup
    dried
1 medium onion, finely chopped
2 cloves garlic, finely chopped
2 tablespoons chopped parsley
½ teaspoon ground rosemary
1 cup dry white wine
1 cup tomato sauce
½ cup water
Salt and pepper to taste

Wash and cut chicken into pieces. Lightly flour chicken pieces. Put oil and butter into a large frying pan. When oil and butter are hot, brown chicken on both sides. Add mushrooms, onions, garlic, parsley and rosemary. Cook 10 minutes. Drain off all the oil, add wine, and cook until wine evaporates. Add tomato sauce, water, salt and pepper. Cover and cook slowly until well done. Decorate with sprigs of parsley and wait 20 minutes before serving.

Serves four.

Capp's Corner Restaurant

1600 Powell Street
San Francisco

Tripe with Potatoes

1½ pounds tripe
1 onion, diced
2 carrots, diced
3 celery stalks, diced
2 cloves garlic, chopped
2 tablespoon olive oil
1 cup canned solid pack tomatoes, chopped
2 cups white wine
3 potatoes, diced
Chicken or beef stock to cover

Boil tripe in plain water for 1½ hours. Drain and cut into strips about ½ inch wide, 3 inches long.

Sauté onions, carrots, celery and garlic in oil cooking until golden brown. Add 1 cup chopped tomatoes and simmer for 5 minutes.

Place tripe in baking pan. Cover with sautéed vegetables and tomatoes.

Place in 500° oven for 10 minutes. Stirring ingredients and add wine and completely cover with chicken or beef stock. Cover pan and reduce heat to hearty simmer. Bake for 2 hours and 30 minutes. Add diced potatoes, season with salt and pepper and cook until potatoes and tripe are tender.

Serves six.

Rice and Clams

To prepare fish stock combine:
2 slices rock cod
½ onion, diced
½ carrot, diced
1 tomato, diced
1 sprig chopped parsley
Juice of ½ lemon
1 glass of white wine
4 quarts water
Salt and pepper to taste

Put all ingredients in a pot, bring to a boil and simmer for one hour.

To prepare rice combine:
1 onion, finely chopped
3 cloves garlic, chopped
1½ cups rice
1 tablespoon butter
1 tablespoon oil
2 glasses white wine
Salt and pepper to taste

Sauté onions, garlic and rice in butter and oil until well browned. Add wine and cook until liquid is absorbed. Cover rice with fish stock and continue simmering. Add more stock if necessary until rice is tender. Season with salt and pepper to taste.

To prepare clams:
4 doz. clams, thoroughly cleaned
1 onion, finely chopped
3 cloves garlic, finely chopped
1 sprig parsley, finely chopped
1 tablespoon butter
1 tablespoon oil
2 glasses white wine

Sauté onion, garlic and parsley in butter and oil. Add clams and wine. Cover and steam until clams open.

Serve over rice.

Serves six.

Castagnola's Restaurant

Jefferson and Jones
Fisherman's Wharf
San Francisco

Calamari Calabresse

 2 pounds calamari
¼ cup olive oil
 1 teaspoon finely chopped parsley
Salt and pepper to taste
Lemon juice (or vinegar) to taste

Clean calamari. Do not cut. Put the whole calamari in water, and boil for 10 minutes. Drain, dry, and put in deep bowl. Add oil, parsley, salt, pepper, and lemon juice or vinegar. Serve hot or cold.
Serves four to six.

Broiled Scallops

16 scallops
 3 tablespoons oil
 1 clove garlic, chopped
Salt and pepper to taste
Lemon, cut in quarters

Put scallops in a pie plate; add oil, garlic, and salt and pepper. Broil for 10 minutes. Then place on platter; add lemon and serve.
Serves two.

Calamari Sicilian Style

Clean calamari and cut into quarters; then fry in olive oil. Add salt and pepper and finely chopped garlic. Do not cook very long (about 10 minutes). When cooked, add parsley. Place on platter. Add lemon juice, to taste, and serve.

Calamari Sautéed

1 pound calamari
4 tablespoons olive oil
½ onion, chopped
6 fresh medium-sized mushrooms, sliced
Salt and pepper to taste
1 large clove garlic, chopped fine
¼ cup sauterne wine

Cut calamari in quarters; simmer in hot frying pan with oil for 2 or 3 minutes. Add onion, mushrooms, garlic, and salt and pepper to taste. Cook for 5 to 7 minutes. Raise flame to very high for 1 minute. Add wine, and let simmer for 2 minutes. Cooking time: 10 to 12 minutes altogether.

Serves two or three.

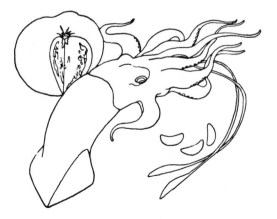

Bar Balued Prawns

12 large prawns
 4 tablespoons oil
 1 clove garlic, chopped
Salt and pepper to taste
 1 lemon, cut in quarters

Put prawns in a pie plate; add oil, garlic, and salt and pepper, and broil for 10 minutes. Place on platter; add lemon and serve.
Serves two.

Crab Creole

1 onion
1 clove garlic
3 pieces celery
2 tablespoons olive oil
Salt and pepper to taste
Flour, to thicken
2 no. 2 cans solid-pack tomatoes
1 no. 2 can tomato purée
Pinch of sweet basil, laurel, rosemary
Few grains of cayenne, paprika
Dash of Worcestershire sauce
1½ cups crabmeat

Dice onion, garlic, and celery. Sauté in olive oil until brown. Add seasonings and enough flour to thicken; then add tomatoes, purée, and herbs. Salt and pepper to taste, and cook 4 hours. When ready to serve, add crab. Cook for 10 minutes.
Makes 1 quart.

Fior D'Italia Restaurant

621 Union Street
San Francisco

Risotto Milanese

4 tablespoons butter
1 medium onion, minced
1½ cups rice
2 quarts chicken broth
¼ cup butter
1 small container saffron dissolved in
   2 tablespoons of broth
½ cup grated Parmesan cheese
½ cup dry white wine

Melt 4 tablespoons of butter in saucepan over moderate heat, add onion. As soon as the onion becomes limp (do not allow it to brown), add wine and allow wine to evaporate. Add rice and stir well until it is coated with butter. Add broth a little at a time. Do not allow rice to become too dry. Cook over a low flame, adding broth a little at a time until rice is done—the time will vary according to whether you like your rice al dente or well done—20 to 30 minutes. Add ¼ cup of butter, the saffron, and mix well. Sprinkle with Parmesan cheese and serve.

Serves three to four.

Stuffed Zucchini

6 medium sized zucchini
3 cups soft bread crumbs
½ cup grated Parmesan cheese
1 green onion
2 cloves garlic
3 tablespoons minced parsley
Salt and pepper to taste
2 beaten eggs
2 tablespoons butter
2 teaspoons majoram

Cook zucchini in salt water (boiling) for 3 minutes. Halve lengthwise, remove pulp with teaspoon. Sauté minced onion, garlic and parsley in butter until browned and add to the pulp, then mix well with bread crumbs, cheese, salt and pepper. Fill zucchini shells with mixture, dot with butter and sprinkle with additional cheese. Bake in moderate oven, 350°, for about 30 minutes.

Serves six.

Fisherman's Grotto

No. 9 Fisherman's Wharf
San Francisco

Cioppino Sauce

½ cup olive oil
1½ cups chopped onions
1 tablespoon chopped garlic
1 tablespoon chopped parsley
1 tablespoon celery
1 tablespoon chopped green bell pepper
2 cups solid-pack tomatoes
1 cup tomato sauce
2 tablespoons salt
1 tablespoon black pepper
1 tablespoon paprika
½ cup sherry wine
3 cups water
Small sprig of fresh basilico

Braise onions, garlic, parsley, celery, and green bell pepper in oil until golden brown. Add tomatoes and tomato sauce, salt, black pepper, paprika, sherry wine, and basilico. Cook 15 minutes. Add water, and cook slowly for 1 hour.

This amount of sauce will serve six. Any fresh fish or shellfish may be used.

Chef's Special Salad Dressing

1½ cups chili sauce
¼ cup finely ground celery
¼ cup finely ground sour pickles
2 cups mayonnaise
1 teaspoon lemon juice
½ teaspoon Worcestershire sauce
1 teaspoon horseradish

Put all ingredients into bowl. Mix until well blended.

When stored in cool place, dressing will keep indefinitely. Do not refrigerate.

This dressing can be used on any seafood salad.

Makes 1 quart.

Franciscan Restaurant

Fisherman's Wharf
San Francisco

Jumbo Prawns Sauté Marsala

1 pound jumbo prawns
2 tablespoons cooking oil
1 chopped green onion
Pinch of whole rosemary
1 clove garlic, chopped
1 chopped white onion
¼ cup Marsala wine
½ cup Brown Sauce
Salt and pepper to taste

Peel and fantail prawns. Sauté in hot oil. Add green onion, rosemary, garlic, white onion, wine, **Brown Sauce** (see page 102), and salt and pepper. Lower heat, and simmer for 10 minutes. This seafood succulence is served with rice pilaff.
Serves two.

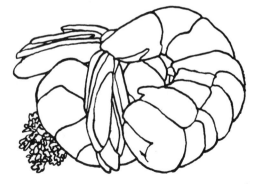

Crab Legs Sauté

4 tablespoons butter
¼ pound sliced mushrooms
1 clove garlic, chopped
2 tablespoons chopped green onions
1 chopped shallot
1½ pounds crab legs
Pinch of white pepper
¼ cup sherry wine
½ pint Brown Sauce

Sauté, in butter, mushrooms, garlic, onions, and shallot until tender (about 5 minutes). Add crab legs, pepper, and wine. Continue to sauté. Reduce sherry until almost dry. Add **Brown Sauce** (see page 102), and simmer until hot and mixed.

Serves six.

Gaylord India Restaurant

900 North Point
Ghirardelli Square
San Francisco

Gaylord Fried Okra with Cumin

2½ tablespoons *ghee* (clarified butter) or
    vegetable oil
1 medium onion, chopped
1 teaspoon salt
1 pound whole fresh okra
2½ teaspoons ground cumin
¼ teaspoon ground black pepper

In a heavy frying pan, heat *ghee* or oil until
very hot. Add onions and salt, and stir for about 7 or 8
minutes until onions are light brown. Add okra,
cumin, and pepper. Cook until okra is tender and
most of the liquid has evaporated. Serve hot.
    Serves four.

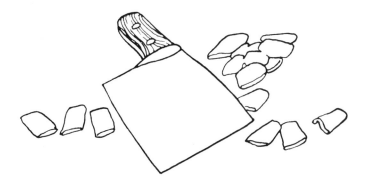

Gaylord Chicken Curry

6 tablespoons vegetable oil
3 pounds chicken, cut into pieces
¾ cup finely chopped onion
2½ teaspoons chopped garlic
1¾ teaspoons finely chopped fresh ginger
1 teaspoon ground cumin
½ teaspoon turmeric
1 teaspoon ground coriander
1 teaspoon cayenne
½ pound chopped tomatoes
1 tablespoon fresh, finely chopped green
   coriander
6 tablespoons unflavored yoghurt
2½ teaspoons salt
½ cup water
2½ teaspoons lemon juice
1 teaspoon *garam masala**

Garam masala is made by grinding finely
together: 1 inch stick cinnamon, 6 green
cardamons, 6 cloves, ½ teaspoon cumin seeds,
¾ teaspoon corianders, and ½ teaspoon black
peppercorn.

(Continued on p. 37)

Hyde Street Cable Car with Alcatraz in background.
Photo © David Ryan/Photo 20–20

Sea Lions (*Zalophus californius*) take over docks at Pier 39.
Photo © David Ryan/Photo 20–20

Coit Tower on Telegraph Hill.
Photo © Ted Streshinsky/Photo 20–20

In a large heavy frying pan, heat oil until it is very hot. Add chicken, and fry for 2 or 3 minutes. Transfer the chicken to a plate. Add onions, garlic, and ginger to the oil remaining in the frying pan, and fry for about 7 or 8 minutes, stirring constantly, until the onions are soft and golden brown. Reduce the heat to low. Add cumin, turmeric, ground coriander, cayenne, and 1 tablespoon water. Fry for 1 minute or so, stirring constantly; then add tomatoes, fresh coriander, yoghurt, and salt. Cook until the oil separates from the mixture. Add the chicken. Pour in the rest of the water. Bring to a boil, turning chicken in the sauce. Cook until chicken is tender. Pour lemon juice over the dish, and sprinkle with *garam masala.* Serve hot.

Serves four to six.

Green Valley Restaurant

510 Green Street
San Francisco

Chicken Polenta

3 chickens cut into 8 pieces each
1½ onion, finely chopped
1 celery heart, finely chopped
2 carrots, finely chopped
3 cloves garlic, finely chopped
1 lb. mushrooms, sliced
1 pint white wine
1 16 oz. can solid pack tomatoes
1 16 oz. can water
Thyme, sage and rosemary to taste
Salt and pepper to taste
2 tablespoon olive oil

Brown chicken on both sides. Sauté onions, celery, carrots, garlic and mushrooms in olive oil. Add to chicken, add wine and sauté for 1 minute. Add tomato, water, salt, pepper, thyme, sage, and rosemary and cook until chicken is tender.

Serves six or eight.

Polenta

½ gal. water
¼ pound butter
1 pint milk
1 lb. corn meal

Boil water. Add polenta, butter, and milk and cook for 2 hours.

When polenta is cooked put some polenta onto individual plates and top with pieces of chicken and sauce.

Serves six or eight.

Hayes Street Grill

324 Hayes Street
San Francisco

Calamari (Squid) Salad

3 pounds fresh calamari (1½ pounds cleaned)
2 thinly sliced red bell peppers
1 small red onion, thinly sliced
½ bunch parsley, finely chopped
6 cloves garlic, finely chopped
3 tablespoons capers
½ cup red wine vinegar
1 cup olive oil
Salt and pepper to taste
Juice of 1 or 2 lemons

Clean and cut calamari into rings, leaving tentacles whole. Drop into rapidly boiling salted water for 15 seconds, just until calamari turns white. If cooked longer, they will turn rubbery. Drain quickly and rinse in cold water. Drain again, and towel dry. Place in bowl; add bell pepper and onion.

Toss with parsley, garlic, capers, vinegar, and oil. Season with salt and pepper. Adjust seasoning with lemon juice.

To clean calamari: Pull out head and tentacles. Cut off tentacles above eyes. Squeeze tentacles to remove spherical bone. Put a finger in the mantle to pull out cellophanelike sword, or cuttle bone. Starting from the pointed tip of body, squeeze out the remaining inters. Wash in running water.

Serves six.

Ceviche

**2 pounds fresh snapper or ling cod, boned and
     cut into small pieces**
Lime and lemon juice
**Small bunch of cilantro (Chinese parsley),
     chopped**
3 chopped ripe tomatoes
1 chopped Bermuda onion
Hot sauce and salt to taste

Marinate fish in a marinade of equal parts of lime
and lemon juice (enough to cover the fish). Marinate
for 8 hours, or overnight. Add to the marinated fish
the cilantro, tomatoes and onions. Season with hot
sauce and salt, and serve.
     Serves four to five.

La Contadina Restaurant

1800 Mason Street
San Francisco

Spaghetti with Calamari

5 pounds calamari, cleaned, cut in medium-sized pieces, and well drained
2 tablespoons garlic oil
¼ onion, finely chopped
2 tablespoons chopped green onions
1 tablespoon chopped fresh parsley
6 tablespoons tomato sauce, fresh homemade if possible
Pinch crushed pepper
¼ cup sliced fresh mushrooms
Salt and pepper
½ cup red wine
Clam juice (see recipe)

Sauté onions, parsley, tomato, crushed red pepper and mushrooms in garlic oil; add tomato sauce and red wine. Allow sauce to cook for 5 minutes.

Add calamari; stir into sauce; add salt and pepper. When calamari comes to a boil, cook uncovered over medium flame for 5 minutes *only* (overcooking will make calamari tough).

Add clam juice to calamari, stir and remove from flame. Keeping calamari sauce in refrigerator overnight improves flavor. Serve hot over freshly cooked pasta.

Garlic Oil

½ **cup** *each* **olive oil and salad oil**
10 cloves garlic

Blend well in electric blender.

Clam Juice

6 hardshell clams
¾ **cup chicken stock**
1 teaspoon chopped green onions
Juice of ¼ lemon
Pinch fresh chopped parsley
1 tablespoon garlic oil
Fresh ground black pepper

Place clams and chicken stock in saucepan. Sprinkle remaining ingredients over clams. Cover, bring to a boil, and cook over medium heat 3–4 minutes until clams begin to open. Add a sprinkle of white wine and 1 tablespoon butter. Cook for 1 more minute, remove from flame. Drain juice to use in calamari recipe. Eat clams.

The Mandarin

900 North Point
Ghirardelli Square
San Francisco

Fillet of Rock Cod with Sweet and Sour Sauce

1 rock cod (about 3 pounds)
2 eggs
2 tablespoons water
Generous splash of sherry
2 heaping tablespoons all-purpose flour
Cornstarch
Cottonseed oil

Slice cod along backbone and below gills. Remove skin. Slice steaks lengthwise into strips, then crosswise into 2-inch segments. Make batter of eggs, water, sherry, and flour. Mix well. Dip cod into batter; then roll in cornstarch.

Heat oil over high temperature until bubbling. Deep fry cod 4 to 5 minutes until golden brown. Remove with strainer, and reserve.

Prepare **Sweet and Sour Sauce** (see recipe below). Refry fillets for 1 to 2 minutes. Drain, and place on platter. Pour sauce over fillets just before serving.

Serves four.

Sweet and Sour Sauce 1

1 cup sugar
1 cup water
½ cup white vinegar
4 tablespoons catsup
1 tablespoon soy sauce
2 tablespoons cornstarch in enough water to
    dissolve

      Cook sugar, water, vinegar, and catsup over
high heat for 2 to 3 minutes. Add soy sauce and
cornstarch/water solution. Stir to blend and thicken.

Scallops Fu Yung

½ pound scallops
 2 cups cottonseed oil
10 egg whites, lightly beaten until foamy
¼ pound bean sprouts
Chicken stock
 3 to 4 scallions (white part only), shredded
    lengthwise
⅓ cup Virginia ham (or other uncooked ham),
    sliced thin and shredded
Pinch of sugar
Pinch of salt
Generous splash of sherry
Pinch of white pepper
Pinch of monosodium glutamate
Few drops of sesame oil
 2 to 3 tablespoons cornstarch in enough water
    to dissolve
Fresh coriander (Chinese parsley)

Gently boil scallops for about 1 hour. Beat with whisk until shredded. Drain off liquid.

Heat oil in wok over medium temperature. Drop in egg whites, and turn off heat. When egg whites fluff up in oil, remove with a strainer. Reserve.

Using a strainer, simmer scallops and bean sprouts in chicken stock for 1 to 2 minutes. Drain.

Heat wok over high temperature. Coat inside surface with very little oil. Add scallions and ham. Toss and stir for 1 to 2 minutes. Then add scallops, bean sprouts, sugar, salt, sherry, white pepper, monosodium glutamate, sesame oil, and cornstarch/water solution, continuing to toss and stir.

Add egg whites. Toss and stir for 1 minute more. Garnish with coriander and serve.

Serves four.

Sweet and Sour Fish

1 rock cod, carp, or red snapper (about 3 pounds)
2 tablespoons soy sauce
2 tablespoons sherry
1 egg
4 tablespoons cornstarch
4 cups vegetable oil
Sweet pepper (optional)
Carrot shreds (optional)

Clean fish, leaving head, tail, and fins intact. Make five or six deep parallel slashes on both sides so sauce will soak into meat. Combine soy sauce, sherry, egg, and cornstarch. Rub mixture on both sides of fish.

Heat oil over high temperature until bubbling. Deep fry fish on both sides until deep golden brown. Remove fish to a long platter. The fish may be fried in advance and refried just before serving to make it crisper.

Prepare Sauce **Sweet and Sour** (see recipe below). Pour sauce over hot fish just before serving. Garnish with sweet pepper and carrot shreds, if desired.

Serves four.

Sweet and Sour Sauce 2

8 tablespoons catsup
4 tablespoons wine vinegar
8 tablespoons sugar
6 tablespoons soy sauce
4 tablespoons cornstarch, mixed with 2 cups
     water

Put catsup, vinegar, sugar, and soy sauce in a pot. Mix and boil for a few minutes. Gradually add cornstarch/water mixture, stirring until a thick sauce results.

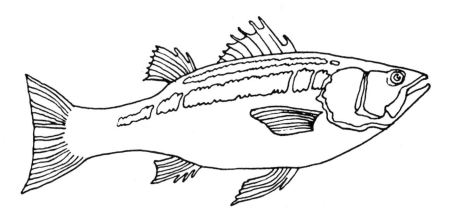

Neptune's Palace

Pier 39
San Francisco

Neptune's Palace Delight

1 pound cream cheese
¼ cup sugar
2 egg yolks
2 tablespoons brandy
¼ cup cream
Fresh fruit
Syrup
Fresh berries purée

Whip cream cheese until nice and light. Add sugar, and cream well until sugar has been absorbed. Add egg yolks one at a time, beating thoroughly after each addition. Flavor with brandy. Mix well. Finish by whipping the cream and adding it to pudding. Blend well for several minutes. Chill for several hours.

Using pastry bag, fill ramekin molds one-third full and chill. Top with fresh fruit in your favorite syrup or purée of fresh berries.

Serves four.

Neptune's Palace Scallops Sauté with Snow Peas

8 or 9 plump scallops, well washed
Clarified butter
2 tablespoons sherry wine
¼ cup heavy cream
6 or 7 snow peas, washed
Salt, pepper, and nutmeg to taste
Fish Stock (optional)

Wash scallops well. Sauté scallops in butter for 2 minutes. Add sherry, stirring constantly. Do not let pan or scallops brown. Add cream, and reduce until sauce is thick and coats the back of a spoon. Add snow peas. Bring to a simmer; season with salt, pepper and nutmeg. Serve hot.

Serves one.

Optional: You may substitute a good **Fish Stock** (see page 102) with sherry already added to it, instead of using just sherry to give the sauce a bit more complexity in taste.

New Pisa Restaurant

550 Green Street
San Francisco

Sausage with Beans and Tomato Sauce

12 Sausages

Boil for 20 minutes with one bay leaf.

Tomato Sauce

2 cups dried beans
1 28 oz. can solid pack tomatoes
1 28 oz. can water
2 cloves garlic, chopped
1 teaspoonful parsley, chopped
1 cup onions, chopped
1 bayleaf
A sprig of rosemary
Salt and pepper to taste

Sauté onions, garlic and parsley in cooking oil. Add tomato, water, rosemary, salt and pepper and bring to a boil. Lower heat and simmer for 1 hour then add beans. Cook until beans are tender, then add sausage and cook for 15 minutes longer. To serve, place two sliced sausages on each platter and top with beans and sauce.
Serves six.

Tripe

2 lbs. tripe, washed
Juice from 1 lemon
6 cloves
1 bay leaf
4 qts. of water

Boil tripe with lemon juice, cloves, and bay leaf until tender. Cut into strips about 3 inches long and ⅜ inch wide.

Tomato Sauce

1 28 oz. can solid pack tomatoes
2 28 oz. cans of water
2 cloves garlic, finely chopped
1 small onion, finely chopped
1 teaspoon chopped parsley
1 sprig of rosemary
1 tablespoon cooking oil
Salt and pepper to taste

Sauté garlic, onion and parsley in cooking oil. Add tomato, water, salt and pepper and bring to a boil. Lower heat and simmer 1 hour. Add tripe and cook for 1 hour more.
Serves six or eight.

North Beach Restaurant

1512 Stockton Street
San Francisco

Pasta Filoso

2 slices of Prosciutto, cut into small pieces
2 slices pork belly, (cold meat), cut into small
   pieces
¼ cup chopped onions
1 clove chopped garlic
2 fresh tomatoes quartered
1 tablespoon sweet butter
2 cups whipping cream
Salt and pepper to taste
1 lb. pasta cooked and drained

Sauté onions and garlic in sweet butter. Add prosciutto and pork belly and sauté for one minute. Add tomatoes, salt and pepper and cook for 10 or 15 minutes. Add cream and cook quickly for a few minutes till the sauce thickens.

After pasta has been cooked place on a platter, pour sauce over pasta, and serve.

Serves four to five.

Old Swiss House

Pier 39
San Francisco

Pgules au Whiskey

8 pieces boneless chicken breast, sliced thin
½ cup butter
1 teaspoon mustard
Pinch of rosemary
2 tablespoons flour
2 tablespoons whiskey
2 tablespoons beef *jus*
1 cup heavy cream
Salt and pepper to taste
½ teaspoon Worcestershire sauce

Sauté chicken in butter for 2 minutes. Add mustard, and mix. Season with a pinch of rosemary, and sprinkle with flour. Flame with whiskey. Add beef *jus* and heavy cream. Season with salt, pepper, and Worcestershire sauce. During the whole process, keep heat rather low.

Serves four.

A. Sabella's Restaurant

Fisherman's Wharf
San Francisco

Stuffed Turbot with Deviled Crab

2 medium mushrooms, sliced
1 clove garlic, crushed
1 chopped shallot
½ pimento, diced
½ teaspoon chopped parsley
1 tablespoon cooking oil
½ pound cooked crabmeat
1 tablespoon brandy
¼ cup sherry wine
½ cup Cream Sauce
1 well-beaten egg
Dash of hot sauce
4 drops Worcestershire sauce
Salt and pepper to taste
4 fillets of turbot
1 cup sherry wine
Salt to taste
Paprika
Drawn butter
Lemon slices

Sauté mushrooms, garlic, shallots, pimento and parsley in oil. Add crabmeat, brandy, 2 ounces sherry wine. **Cream Sauce** (see page 101), egg, hot sauce, and Worcestershire sauce. Season with salt and pepper. Mix together well. Cook for 10 minutes.

Place two fillets in a well-buttered baking pan. Put half of the crab mix on each fillet. Top each with another fillet. Press down firmly with hands, and lock with toothpicks so fillets will not come apart while cooking.

The turbot is now ready for the oven. Pour 1 cup sherry wine over turbot; sprinkle lightly with salt. Sprinkle with paprika. Pour melted butter over each turbot, and garnish with a slice of lemon. Bake in 400-degree oven for 20 to 25 minutes. Baste frequently.

Serves two.

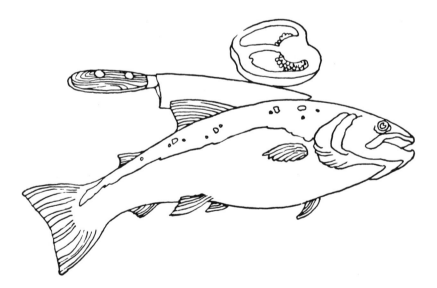

Crabmeat with Spaghetti

1 cup chopped onions
1 teaspoon chopped garlic
1 teaspoon chopped parsley
1 teaspoon chopped celery
4 tablespoons olive oil
1 cup solid-pack tomatoes
1½ cups water
2 teaspoons salt
1 teaspoon black pepper
1 pound fresh crabmeat
¼ cup sherry wine
1 pound spaghetti
½ teaspoon paprika
Grated Parmesan cheese

Sauté onions, garlic, parsley, and celery in olive oil until golden brown. Add solid-pack tomatoes, water, salt, and pepper. Simmer over low flame for 1 hour. Add crabmeat and wine, and simmer for another 10 minutes.

Cook and drain spaghetti. Place on platter. Pour sauce with crabmeat over spaghetti. Top with Parmesan cheese. Sprinkle with paprika. Serve hot.

Serves five.

Stuffed Swordfish Antone

2 center slices swordfish
½ cup chopped onions
1 tablespoon oil
1 cup shrimp
1 cup cooked chopped spinach
2 cups milk

Dash of cayenne
Pinch of dry mustard
½ teaspoon chopped parsley
1 tablespoon Worcestershire sauce
¼ cup sherry wine
Salt and pepper to taste
4 tablespoons flour
4 tablespoons melted butter
¼ cup chopped pimento

Sauté onion. Add shrimp and spinach. Cook 5 minutes. Add milk, then cayenne, mustard, parsley, Worcestershire sauce, and sherry wine. Bring to boil. Mix with salt, pepper, flour, and butter. Cook until thickened, stirring constantly.

Roll deviled shrimp inside two slices of swordfish. Bake 20 minutes.

Place in casserole. Cover with **Sauce Supreme** (see recipe below). Garnish with chopped pimento and grated cheese. Bake 20 minutes at 350 degrees.

Serves two.

Sauce Supreme

4 drops hot sauce
1 cup clam broth
2 tablespoons white wine

Add the above ingredients to basic white sauce.

Sabella and La Torre

Fisherman's Wharf
San Francisco

Crab Newburg Supreme

2 tablespoons butter
1 tablespoon minced onion
Green pepper
1 tablespoon parsley
1 cup sliced mushrooms
2 tablespoons flour
1¾ cups milk
¼ cup sherry
½ teaspoon oregano
½ teaspoon thyme
Salt and pepper to taste
2 cups crabmeat
2 egg yolks

Melt butter in saucepan. Add onion, parsley, green pepper, and mushrooms. Cover, and cook gently for 10 minutes. Blend in flour, add milk, and continue cooking, stirring constantly, until mixture thickens. Add all other ingredients, and heat.

Serve in patty shells or on toast.

Serves two.

Shrimp Rarebit

5 tablespoons butter
7 tablespoons flour
2 cups milk
4 ounces shredded sharp cheddar cheese
1 tablespoon prepared mustard
1 level teaspoon salt
Pepper to taste
Dash of Worcestershire sauce
½ cup beer
Dash of cayenne
2 tablespoons mayonnaise
2 cups cooked shrimp

Melt butter, stir in flour, add milk and cheese. Cook, stirring constantly. Add all other ingredients except shrimp, and blend thoroughly. Add shrimp. Heat well.

Serve on buttered toast.

Serves two to four.

Prawns Patriced

4 stalks sliced celery
1 medium onion, sliced
1 large green pepper, sliced
1 clove garlic, minced
4 strips bacon, chopped
2 tablespoons olive oil
½ cup tomato purée
Juice of one lemon
2 pounds raw prawns, peeled
4 tomatoes, peeled and diced
Dash of hot sauce
1 tablespoon chopped parsley
2 tablespoons Worcestershire sauce
¼ cup sherry

Sauté celery, onion, pepper, garlic, and bacon in oil. Add tomato purée, lemon juice, and prawns, and simmer for 10 minutes. Add all other ingredients. Thicken slightly with cornstarch.

Serve with boiled or steamed rice.

Serves four.

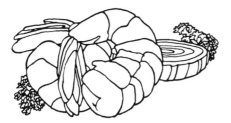

Salmon à l'Orlando

2-ounce can anchovy fillets
2 tablespoons olive oil
1 clove garlic, minced
¼ cup sherry wine
Chopped parsley
Juice of 1 lemon
2 pounds sliced salmon
Salt and pepper to taste

Drain oil from anchovies into pan. Add olive oil and garlic, and cook anchovies to a paste. Add wine, parsley, and lemon juice. Place salmon in baking pan; salt and pepper. Pour mixture over salmon. Bake about ½ hour at 400 degrees.

Serves four.

Sam's Grill and Seafood Restaurant

374 Bush
San Francisco

Clams Elizabeth

1 dozen medium clams
1 tablespoon finely chopped chives or scallions
2 tablespoons fine bread crumbs
1 tablespoon grated Parmesan cheese
Juice of 1 lemon
2 tablespoons melted butter
¼ cup sherry wine
Paprika

Use any clams in season. Open each clam, leaving the clam in one half of the shell. Reserve the juice. Place the clams in a shallow dish. Pour a small amount of juice on each clam, and sprinkle with chives or scallions. Mix bread crumbs and cheese, and sprinkle lightly over each clam. Pour the lemon juice, then the butter, over all, and add the sherry wine around the edge. Cover lightly with paprika. Bake in a hot oven (400 degrees) for 20 minutes, or until brown.

Serves one.

Deviled Crab à la Sam

6 stalks of celery, without leaves
2 medium onions
1 large green pepper
1½ cups vegetable oil
2 cups flour
Dash of ground white pepper
Dash of ground nutmeg
3 teaspoons dry mustard
1½ quarts scalded milk
2 pounds fresh crabmeat
Grated Parmesan cheese
Dash of paprika
Melted butter

Chop celery, onions, and green pepper very fine. Cook slowly in oil until tender (about 10 minutes). Stirring constantly, sprinkle and add flour, white pepper, nutmeg, and mustard. Keep stirring until smooth and bubbling. Still stirring constantly, add hot scalded milk; continue stirring fast till sauce is thick and smooth. Add crabmeat. (If you use canned crabmeat, drain off all juice before adding to sauce.) Stir well, and cook until it starts to boil; remove from fire. Heat oven to 400 degrees. Pour crab with sauce into ovenproof casserole or serving dish. Sprinkle generously with Parmesan cheese, add a dash of paprika, and dribble with melted butter. Bake in oven until golden brown (about 5 minutes).

Serves four.

Hangtown Fry

25 to 30 baby oysters
Flour
Eggwash (1 beaten egg with 1 teaspoon milk)
Bread crumbs
Oil for deep frying
  2 tablespoons butter or margarine
  2 or 3 eggs
  2 slices bacon

Roll oysters in flour, so they are well coated. Dip into eggwash; then roll in fine bread crumbs. Deep fry in oil; drain and put aside.

Melt butter in frying pan; whip the eggs, and pour into frying pan. Stir slightly, and add prepared oysters while eggs are still half done so that they will bind the oysters. Flip omelette, and cook on other side. In the meantime, cook bacon in second pan. When omelette and bacon are done (it should be at the same time), slip the omelette onto platter and top with the cooked bacon. Serve immediately.

Serves one.

Scoma's

Pier 47
Fisherman's Wharf
San Francisco

Sole Fish à la Via Reggio

½ medium onion, chopped
 1 clove garlic, minced
Sliced fresh mushrooms
Pinch oregano
½ cup white wine
 2 or 3 tablespoons solid-pack tomatoes, ground
 1 tablespoon tomato paste
 1 cup water
 1 pound sole
Chopped fresh spinach
Salt and pepper to taste

Sauté onion, garlic, and mushrooms in small amount of oil until onion turns golden. Add oregano, wine, tomatoes, tomato paste, and water. Cook this sauce for 5 minutes. Add sole. Cook over low heat for 15 minutes. A few minutes before fish is cooked, add chopped fresh spinach. Season.

Serves two.

Canneloni (with Seafood Filling)

½ medium onion, chopped
½ clove garlic, chopped
Sliced fresh mushrooms
Oil
 1 tablespoon white wine
 1 cup Supreme Sauce
½ pound crabmeat
½ pound shrimp meat
Parmesan cheese
Sliced Monterey Jack cheese

Prepare **Napolitana Sauce** (see recipe below). As it simmers, prepare **Supreme Sauce** (see recipe below). Set aside.

Sauté onion, garlic, and mushrooms in a small amount of oil. Add wine, Supreme Sauce, crab, shrimp, and a pinch of Parmesan cheese. Stir. Allow filling to cool.

Prepare crepe batter (using any standard recipe). In a lightly greased pan, cook 1 tablespoon of batter for 1 minute on each side. Place 1 tablespoon of filling on each crepe. Roll.

In a large baking pan, put ½ cup Napolitana Sauce. Place the filled canneloni in the pan. Put in preheated, 350-degree oven for 3 to 4 minutes. Remove pan from oven. Top each canneloni with a pinch of Parmesan cheese and a slice of Monterey Jack cheese.

Return pan to oven. The canneloni are ready to serve when the cheese topping has melted.

Serves four.

Napolitana Sauce

1 medium onion, chopped
4 cloves garlic, chopped
Oil
Pinch of oregano
3 to 4 bay leaves
1 no. 10 can solid-pack tomatoes, ground
1 tablespoon tomato paste
1 cup water
Salt to taste
Pinch of chili pepper
Sugar, as needed

Sauté onion and garlic in oil. Season with oregano and bay leaves. When onion turns golden, add tomatoes, tomato paste, and water. Simmer for ½ hour. Add sugar to reduce acidity.

Supreme Sauce

1 cup butter
1 cup flour
6 cups hot milk

Melt butter in a pan. Blend in flour, stirring over low heat (all flour must be blended with the butter for a smooth sauce).

Stir in the milk. Season with salt. Cook for approximately 3 minutes, stirring so the sauce is smooth.

San Francisco Victorians with
TransAmerica Pyramid in background.
Photo © Ted Streshinsky/Photo 20–20

Fisherman's Wharf and Golden Gate
Bridge.
Photo © Ted Streshinsky/Photo 20–20

Sea Lion invasion at Pier 39.
Photo © Roberto Soncin Gerometta/
Photo 20–20

Abalone Bordelaise

1 pound abalone
Flour
2 or 3 beaten eggs
1 cup oil

Dip abalone in flour and then in eggs. Heat oil in a frying pan until it is hot. Fry abalone for approximately 1 minute on each side.

Pour **Bordelaise Sauce** (see recipe below) over it. Serve.

Serves two to three.

Bordelaise Sauce

½ medium onion, chopped fine
1 clove garlic, minced
1 tablespoon white wine
½ cup Supreme Sauce
Lemon juice

Sauté onion and garlic in a little oil until onion turns golden. Squeeze lemon juice over the onion and garlic. Add wine and **Supreme Sauce** (see recipe on page 68). Stir over low heat.

Scott's Seafood Grill and Bar

---

3 Embarcadero Center
2400 Lombard
San Francisco

Broiled Salmon

Select a nice pink salmon fillet with a firm texture. Preheat the broiler section of the oven. Brush the fillet with oil or melted butter, season with salt and pepper, and place on broiler pan. Broil under broiler flame for 4 to 5 minutes on each side. Allow 10 minutes cooking time per inch of thickness of fillet.

If salmon fillets are too thick, broil on both sides, then place on well-greased pan with some water or fish stock and continue cooking in moderate oven. Remove salmon skin. Serve immediately with **Hollandaise Sauce** (see page 101).

Fisherman's Stew

2 medium carrots
1 large leek
2 stalks celery
¼ pound mushrooms
2-3 medium cloves garlic, finely chopped
½ pound prawns, peeled and deveined
½ pound scallops (cut in ½ if using large sea
    scallops)
1 pound thick fish fillet (such as rock cod), cut
    into 1-inch-thick cubes
8 cherrystone clams, washed and opened

2 quarts Fish Stock
1 cup white wine
4 ounces bay shrimp
4 ounces crabmeat
8 ounces whole butter
2 lemons, cut into crowns
Chopped parsley

Prepare in individual stew pots or one large pot. If serving in individual stew pots, divide the ingredients by four, and place proper amount in each pot.

Wash and slice vegetables to ¼ inch thick. Place them in stew pot along with garlic, prawns, scallops, fish fillets, clams, **Fish Stock** (see page 102), and wine. Cover, and bring to a boil. Reduce heat. Simmer gently until fish is just cooked (about 6 minutes). Add crabmeat, shrimp, and butter. Continue to simmer until the crab and shrimp are heated through and the butter is melted.

Note: If using one large pot, heat shrimp and crab separately in some fish stock and white wine, and portion into individual serving bowls as garnish.

Garnish with ½ lemon cut into a crown and dusted in chopped parsley. Serve immediately.

Serves four.

Swiss Louis Restaurant

Pier 39
San Francisco

Frittata à la Louis

4 tablespoons butter
1 finely chopped white onion
½ bell pepper, finely chopped
9 beaten eggs
6 ounces finely chopped cooked spinach
½ cup Parmesan cheese
Salt and pepper to taste
8 ounces finely chopped ham

Melt butter in frying pan over medium flame. Add onion and bell pepper; brown lightly. Add mixture of eggs, spinach, cheese, ham, and salt and pepper. Cover, and cook for 2 to 3 minutes, or more if needed. Remove from pan. Cut into quarters. Serve.
Serves four.

Rex Sole Meunière with Capers

4 Rex sole

Clean and flour sole. Grill over low heat. Place two Rex sole in each dish. Pour over **Meunière Sauce** (see recipe below). Top with chopped parsley, and serve.

Serves two.

Meunière Sauce

4 tablespoons butter
Juice of 1 lemon
½ cup white wine
1 tablespoon vinegar
1 tablespoon capers
Sprig of parsley, finely chopped
Salt, pepper, and monosodium glutamate to
taste

Melt butter in frying pan over very hot flame. Add lemon juice, wine, vinegar, and capers. Add salt, pepper, and monosodium glutamate when all ingredients are hot.

Pesto Sauce

 2 cups fresh basil leaves
¼ cup fresh parsley
 1 cup pine nuts or walnuts
 2 cloves garlic, chopped fine
Monosodium glutamate to taste
Salt to taste
 3 cups olive oil
Muffin paper cups

Finely grind basil, parsley, nuts, garlic, and oil. Then mix salt and monosodium glutamate. Fill muffin cups ¾ full, and freeze mixture. When partially frozen, pour oil to top of paper cup and freeze. Leave in freezer until ready to use.

Use over hot noodles or pasta.

Tripe

2 pounds tripe
2 lemons, quartered

Boil tripe with lemons for 1½ hours. Run hot water over tripe to get fat off. Then run cool water over tripe. Cut into ½-inch-by-2-inch strips. Make **Tomato Sauce** (see recipe below). Add tripe to sauce with potatoes, and cook until potatoes are tender.

Serves four.

Tomato Sauce

4 tablespoons butter
1 finely chopped onion
2 stalks celery, finely chopped
1 clove garlic, finely chopped
1 14-ounce can solid-pack tomatoes
1¾ cups water
1 tablespoon salt pork
1 cup beef broth
1 cup white wine
Salt and pepper to taste
2 diced potatoes
Monosodium glutamate to taste

Melt butter in frying pan over medium flame. Add onions, celery, and garlic. Brown lightly. Add tomatoes, water, salt pork, salt and pepper, and monosodium glutamate. Simmer for 10 minutes. Then add broth and wine, and simmer for ½ hour. Add potatoes, and cook until they are tender.

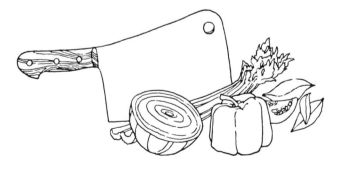

Wild Duck

1 wild duck
1 celery stalk
1 apple
1 tablespoon oil
¼ cup white wine
 4 tablespoons butter
Salt and pepper to taste
 1 teaspoon lemon juice
 1 teaspoon A-1 sauce
 1 teaspoon catsup
 1 shot brandy
 1 shot Kirsch Crème de Almond
½ teaspoon chopped parsley

Stuff wild duck with chunks of celery and apples. Bake at 550 degrees for 15 minutes. Remove from oven, and quickly carve the breast out. Put the breast in skillet with a little oil. Fry 30 seconds on each side. Add white wine.

In a large skillet, place butter, salt and pepper, lemon juice, A-1 sauce, catsup, brandy, and Kirsch Crème de Almond. Keep stirring until sauce is hot. The sauce should be tangy and not too sweet. Put duck breast on plate. Pour sauce over duck. Top with parsley.

Serves two.

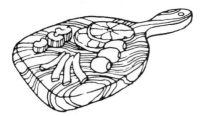

Tarantino's Restaurant

206 Jefferson
Fisherman's Wharf
San Francisco

Crab and Turbot

½ cup Cream Sauce
1 tablespoon Worcestershire sauce
2 tablespoons dry mustard
3 tablespoons French mustard
½ teaspoon chopped shallots
¼ cup chopped pimentos
4 chopped hardboiled eggs
1 pound crabmeat
Salt and pepper to taste
8 slices turbot or fillet of sole

Make **Cream Sauce** (see page 101) of medium thickness, and bring to a boil. Add Worcestershire sauce, both mustards, a little at a time, shallots, pimentos, eggs, crabmeat, and salt and pepper to taste.

Place the turbot slices in a buttered casserole. Pour sauce and crabmeat over fish. Bake in 400-degree oven for 20 to 25 minutes.

Serves four.

Tarantino's Lazy Man's Cioppino

1 pound crabmeat
6 large shrimp, cooked
10 Eastern oysters
10 clams, if available

Place in **Cioppino Sauce** (see recipe below). Simmer for 10 minutes. Serve in casserole or deep dish with hot, buttered garlic toast.
Serves five.

Cioppino Sauce

¼ pound butter
6 finely chopped leeks
3 finely chopped onions
3 finely chopped green peppers
6 stalks celery, chopped fine
1 tablespoon finely chopped garlic
¼ teaspoon whole thyme
¼ teaspoon rosemary
1 cup dry white wine
1 no. 10 can solid-pack tomatoes
1 quart water
Salt and pepper to taste

Sauté in butter (but do not brown) the finely chopped vegetables and spices.
Add tomatoes, wine, and water, and salt and pepper to vegetables. Cook until reduced one quarter.

Tokyo Sukiyaki

225 Jefferson
Fisherman's Wharf
San Francisco

Teriyaki

Teriyaki is broiled pieces of marinated meat or shellfish.

Teriyaki Sauce

1 cup Japanese soy sauce
3 tablespoons granulated sugar
½ cup Mirin (sweet rice wine)
1 teaspoon monosodium glutamate

Mix all ingredients together.

Sukiyaki

1 large piece beef suet (fat)
1 pound beef (boned prime rib, sliced one-eighth
    inch thick in reasonable-sized pieces)
1 bunch fresh green onions (cut in 2-inch
    lengths)
1 piece onion
4 medium-sized fresh mushrooms, sliced
¼ piece *tofu* (soy bean cake), cut into pieces
    approximately 1-by-1½-inches
¼ pound *shirataki* (fine vermicelli-like threads of
    gelatinous starch)
1 piece bamboo shoot
2 medium-sized eggs

Prepare **Sukiyaki Sauce** (see recipe below).
Set aside.

Place a heavy, shallow saucepan on the fire.
Allow it to heat up. Place beef suet in pan to grease it
well. Take out used fat.

Spread slices of beef on the sizzling pan. Brown
slightly to rare. Add onions, vegetables, mushrooms,
tofu, shirataki, and bamboo shoot in that order.
(Theoretically, the longer-to-cook ingredients are
placed in the pan first.)

Quickly add Sukiyaki Sauce (use additional
sugar to suit the taste.) When the host is adept in
cooking sukiyaki, no other liquid need be used, since
the water content of the vegetables produces enough
moisture. However, if while cooking, the pan becomes
too dry, add reasonable amounts of broth to make a
light cooking sauce.

Cook for a few minutes, and the sukiyaki is
ready. Sukiyaki may be dipped in a beaten raw egg to
cool it before eating.

Sukiyaki Sauce 1

½ cup Japanese soy sauce
2 tablespoons granulated sugar
4 tablespoons *sake*
½ cup beef broth

Mix all ingredients together.

Sukiyaki Sauce 2

5 cups beef broth
2 cups Japanese soy sauce
3 tablespoons granulated sugar
½ cup *sake*
3 tablespoons monosodium glutamate

Mix all ingredients together.

Tempura

Tempura is deep-fried, batter-coated pieces of seafood or vegetables.

Fill skillet with vegetable oil 2 inches deep. Set temperature control at 350 degrees. Dip vegetable pieces or seafood bits individually into **Tempura Batter** (see recipe below) and then in hot oil. Time for cooking depends on each ingredient.

Ingredients should be removed just before they are thoroughly cooked. Serve with **Tempura Sauce** (see recipe below).

Tempura Batter

1 egg
½ cup water
1 cup flour

Beat egg well. Add water and flour. Stir lightly.

Tempura Sauce

5 cups bonito soup
1 cup Japanese soy sauce
½ cup *sake*
5 tablespoons granulated sugar
1 tablespoon monosodium glutamate

Mix all ingredients together.

Vannelli's Seafood

Pier 39
San Francisco

Vannelli's Fisherman's Stew

1 large diced onion
1 cup mushrooms, cut into quarters
1 cup diced celery
1 tablespoon chopped parsley
1 level tablespoon finely chopped shallots
2 cups Burgundy wine
½ cup melted butter
1 cup diced tomatoes
4 cloves garlic, finely chopped
Bay leaf, thyme, salt, black pepper, and cayenne
    pepper to taste
16 clams
32 prawns (21 to 24 per pound)
8 medium-sized scallops
8 calamari, cleaned, cut, and parboiled
4 ounces salmon, cut into 1-ounce cubes
4 ounces halibut, cut into 1-ounce cubes
Fish Stock or water

Wilt all vegetables in butter. Add tomatoes
and herbs and seasonings. Then add all the fish,
wine, and enough **Fish Stock** (see page 102) or water
to cover all ingredients. Bring to a boil over low heat.
Simmer for 10 minutes. Serve with garlic bread.
Serves four.

The Waterfront Restaurant

Pier 7
San Francisco

Thrasher Shark, Sautéed and Capered

Cooking oil
24 ounces thrasher shark
Salt and white pepper to taste
½ cup white wine
3 tablespoons capers
3 tablespoons caper vinegar
Butter, to taste
Chopped parsley

Heat cooking oil, and sauté shark about 3 minutes on each side, or until fish flakes separate easily when gently probed with a fork. Salt and pepper both sides of fish. Pour off oil; add white wine, capers, caper vinegar, butter, and parsley. Heat and serve.

Serves four.

California Rock Cod

24 ounces rock cod fillets
Salt and pepper to taste
Flour, as needed
 1 mashed avocado
Lemon juice
Teleme cheese, sliced

Season fillets with salt and pepper. Dust with flour. Sauté lightly in oil until cooked through and browned (approximately 4 minutes). Season mashed avocado with salt, pepper, and lemon juice. Spread cooked fish with avocado. Top with slices of cheese. Place under the broiler until cheese is melted.

Serves four.

Crayfish

 1 stalk celery
 1 carrot
 1 onion
½ clove garlic
48 crayfish
Mustard, mayonnaise, lettuce
½ lemon, sliced

Bring vegetables to a boil in a gallon of water. Boil 15 minutes. Add crayfish, and bring to a second boil. Boil 3 minutes or until red. Remove crayfish. Cool in ice water. Serve on a bed of lettuce with mustard, mayonnaise, and lemon slices.

Serves four.

Yet Wah Mandarin Cuisine

Pier 39
San Francisco

Lemon Chicken Yet Wah Style

2 whole chicken breasts, skinned and boned
1 teaspoon oil
1 teaspoon cornstarch
2 tablespoons oil
½ teaspoon salt
1 teaspoon soy sauce
1 celery stalk, cut diagonally in 1-inch sections
½ green pepper, seeded and cut in ½-inch
   squares
½ red pepper, seeded and cut in ½-inch squares
1 carrot, peeled and cut diagonally in ¼-inch
   slices
2 tablespoons green peas
4 red maraschino cherries, halved
1 teaspoon lemon juice
¼ teaspoon sugar
¼ teaspoon monosodium glutamate (optional)
½ cup pineapple-orange juice
4 slices lemon
2 teaspoons cornstarch
1 tablespoon water

Cut chicken into 1-inch squares. Mix together with 1 teaspoon oil and cornstarch. Allow chicken to marinate in this mixture while you prepare the other ingredients (or for at least 15 minutes).

Place skillet or wok over high heat. When pan is hot, add 2 tablespoons oil. Add the chicken, salt, and soy sauce. Stir fry for 1 minute. Add the vegetables, cherries, lemon juice, sugar, monosodium glutamate, pineapple-orange juice, and lemon slices. Cover the pan. Cook over medium heat for 2 minutes.

Blend cornstarch and water to form a paste, and stir in to thicken the sauce.

Serves four as a main course, or six to eight as part of a complete Chinese meal.

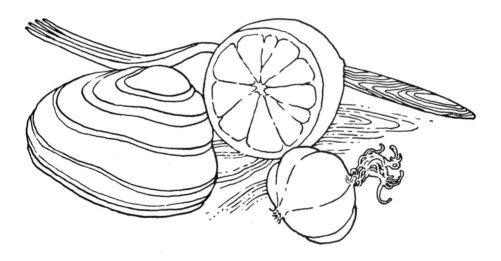

Yet Wah Special Lamb

⅔ pound boned shoulder or leg of lamb, cut in
    ⅛-inch diagonal slices
2 teaspoons cornstarch
2 tablespoons oil
¼ cup shredded carrots
¼ cup bamboo shoots
3 green onions, sliced
½ cup shredded Chinese cabbage
½ teaspoon salt
½ teaspoon sugar
Rice stick noodles
1 sliced green onion

    Sprinkle lamb with cornstarch, and rub into
the meat. Prepare **Yet Wah Special Lamb Sauce**
(see recipe below), and place it near the stove. Place
wok or skillet over high heat; when very hot, add
1 tablespoon oil. Add carrots, bamboo shoots, green
onions, Chinese cabbage, salt, and sugar. Stir fry for
3 minutes, and remove to a plate.

    Pour remaining tablespoon of oil into wok or
skillet. Add lamb. Stir fry for 2 minutes, add sauce,
and cook for a minute longer. Return vegetables to
the wok, and cook briefly to heat vegetables through.

    Serve Yet Wah Special Lamb on a bed of rice
stick noodles, briefly deep fried in hot oil and
removed with a slotted spoon. Place the Yet Wah
Special Lamb on the crisp noodles. Garnish with
slivered green onions.

    Serves two as a main course, or four to six as
part of a complete Chinese meal.

Yet Wah Special Lamb Sauce

¼ teaspoon salt
¼ teaspoon monosodium glutamate (optional)
¼ teaspoon sugar
½ teaspoon soy sauce
½ teaspoon cornstarch
 2 teaspoons Hoisin sauce
 1 teaspoon plum sauce
 1 teaspoon tomato sauce
½ teaspoon oyster sauce

Mix all ingredients together.

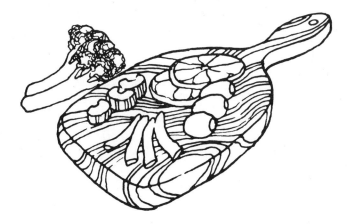

Dalmatian Fish Cookery

The Dalmatian tradition of fish cookery, born along the coast of the Adriatic Sea in Yugoslavia, has been to obtain fish that is almost flopping fresh, then cook it precisely to that evasive instant which barely divides unappetizing translucency from desiccation — and to cook it relatively plainly.

What you then taste, be it sole, salmon, or sea bass, is a flaky flesh with a delicate flavor. There is never a sauce or herb so strong that it covers up the natural flavor — just a sprinkling of parsley and perhaps a bit of lemon and butter.

Sounds ordinary? Just try to achieve that kind of sensitivity at home!

In the waning decades of the Austro-Hungarian empire, while fighting the Turks, the Hapsburg reign exploited what is now Yugoslavia through taxation and conscription. Under such pressures, inhabitants of the agriculturally impoverished Dalmatian coast suffered deprivation. Hence the great migration of the nineteenth and twentieth centuries.

Many of the Dalmatians had been fishermen, so it was natural for them to follow the same occupation once they reached America or to establish restaurants serving fish, the principal source of protein in the old country.

If they failed to call their restaurants Yugoslavian, this lapse was easily explained, since the nation of that name did not come into existence until the end of World War I, in 1918. Indeed, the restaurateurs seemed to go out of their way to take on an American image. While serving up blue-plate specials and merchant lunches, the Dalmatians may have failed to realize the extent of their own contribution.

Because their soil was unproductive, the Dalmatians were obliged to seek their food from the sea. The Dalmatian was more of a seafarer than even the neighboring Italian. The Yugoslavian coastline has many islands and inlets which historically have provided harbors of refuge against Adriatic storms — harbors the Italian coast lacks.

The catch was so precious, moreover, that people prepared it with utmost care. "Care" in this context means a caution against overcooking, which deprives fish of texture as well as taste.

The traditional methods of cooking the fish were plain ones such as charcoal broiling (*gradele*) and poaching. With their proximity to the Adriatic, the Dalmatians were able to feast on fish so fresh that they had no reason to disguise it with sauces or seasonings.

In San Francisco, the Dalmatians established their predominance in catching. Historian Adam S. Eterovich believes that more than two hundred and fifty Dalmatian fishermen lived in San Francisco in the 1870s. According to the California Historical Society, the Fisherman's Wharf Protective Association was headed by a Dalmatian in 1877, 1881, and again in 1884.

Four major fish restaurants in San Francisco (and various chefs in the kitchens of others) have carried on the Dalmatian tradition. At Tadich's (240 California Street), John V. Tadich, a native of Starigrad, took on a second cook, Dominic Ivelich, in 1912. Ivelich recalls that the old man took raw fillets of fish around to tables to sell customers on their freshness. He was so eager to please that if he lacked the fish he would undertake a special shopping expedition to the fish company across the street.

Present owners Steve and Bob Buich are the sons of Louis Buich, one of three brothers to immigrate from the Dalmatian coast and share ownership of Tadich's.

Sam's Grill (see page 63) was named for Sam Zenovich, who came from the Montenegro end of the Dalmatian coast. Its present owners are Walter and his father Gary Seput, son of Walter Seput, Sr., a Dalmatian who took over the restaurant in 1937.

Maye's Oyster House (1233 Polk Street) has been in Slav hands for more than seventy years, according to present owners Ned Boban, Dave Berosh, and Tony Simini. Boban was born in Dalmatia; Berosh is the son of a Dalmatian.

Chris Kriletich, a native of the island of Kortula on the Adriatic Coast, founded Chris's Seafood (694 Mission Street) in 1918. His widow, Onorina Kriletich, owned the restaurant until it was taken over by her daughter, Pat Kriletich.

Some general rules for cooking in the Dalmatian mode, according to the chefs at Tadich's and Chris's: "The simpler we make the fish, the better it comes out," and, "Always undercook. Never overcook. And serve immediately." Another chef adds, "Fish is fish. There are no recipes."

Some things chefs won't tell about their cooking. But some of the less secret ways are revealed in the following recipes.

Adapted from Gerald Adams, "A Special Way with Fish," *California Living Magazine,* February 1, 1976, pp. 25–31.

Sand Dabs and Rex Sole, Fried on a Grill

Clean and de-head fish. Dip in cracker meal or flour and place on a flat grill, medium hot (375 degrees), on a little vegetable oil, which can be seasoned with paprika, salt, and pepper, or lard.

Cook 3 to 5 minutes per side. Debone the fish by whacking off the tail with an extra stiff spatula, then running spatula along either side of backbone. If flesh seems too moist or translucent, place fillets in warm (not hot) oven for a minute or two. Figure three sand dabs or two sole per person.

Dominic Ivelich's Fried Sand Dabs

Ivelich, now retired from Tadich's, likes to cook all fish in a ridge-bottomed cast-iron pan broiler. He pre-heats the pan for 5 minutes, rolls the sand dabs in flour seasoned with salt, pepper, and paprika, then fries the fish without oil over medium heat, 5 minutes per side.

Charcoal Broiled Fish

This method of cooking fish dishes is traditional on the Dalmatian coast.

At the San Francisco Dalmatian restaurants using this method, chefs use Mexican charcoal because they say it retains heat better than briquettes. They ignite the coals at least one hour before cooking time. No trace of flame remains. The coals are both a glowing red and gray in color.

For sea bass, use a steak 1 to 2 inches thick; dip in vegetable oil mixed with paprika, salt, and pepper. For a thicker slice, grill up to 10 minutes each side, 3 or 4 inches above the coals; a shorter time and closer to the coals if thinner. If you're afraid that fish will burn or dry out if kept too long on the coals, place fish in a 400-degree oven for the final 5 minutes, using a pan to which you have added a couple tablespoons of fresh lemon juice.

For salmon steaks: 5 minutes per side for a 1-inch thick steak. For rex sole (whole, in skin): about 3 minutes per side. For swordfish: 5 minutes per side. Times vary slightly according to the heat of the coals and proximity of grate.

Boiled Sea Bass Dalmatian

The classic method of cooking fish, other than the *gradele* or charcoal broiled method, is that of boiling. Actually the fish is simmered gently in a simple court bouillon.

Dominic Ivelich's Boiled Sea Bass Dalmatian

Water sufficient to cover fish in saucepan
1 clove garlic
2 bunches green onions, cut up
1 stalk celery, diced
Salt to taste
Potatoes (optional)
2 bass steaks, weighing ½ pound each

Simmer the water with all ingredients except fish for ½ hour; add fish. Cover, and cook until fish flakes at the touch of a fork — 10 or more minutes, figuring 10 minutes per inch of thickness. Serve with lemon.

Ned Boban's Boiled Sea Bass Dalmatian

Juice of ½ lemon
2 cups water
2 stalks celery, cut up
1 onion, cut in half
Dash of olive oil
Salt and pepper to taste
1 tomato, chopped (optional)
1 or 2 thick slices fresh sea bass

Combine all items but sea bass in a saucepan. Simmer 20 to 30 minutes. Add fish and simmer, covered, until done — 10 minutes or more. Figure 10 minutes per inch of thickness.

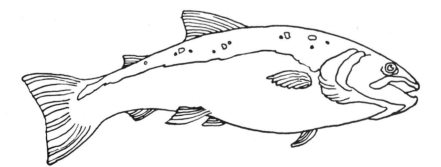

Ernie Aviani's Cioppino

1 onion, sliced
1 clove garlic, chopped
Olive oil, to brown onion and garlic
 2 tablespoons red wine vinegar
 1 live crab, disjointed
12 uncooked prawns
12 fresh clams
 1 can solid-pack tomatoes (large size)
Salt and pepper to taste
¼ teaspoon celery salt
Dash of paprika
Dry sherry to taste
 4 slices fresh sea bass
 1 cup chopped parsley

Sauté onion and garlic in olive oil. When golden, add wine vinegar. Simmer one minute, then add crab, prawns, and clams. Sauté on low flame for 10 minutes, stirring occasionally. Add tomatoes, salt, pepper, celery salt, paprika, and sherry to your taste. Bring to simmer, add fish, cover, and cook 15 minutes, or until fish is done. Top with parsley. Serve with French bread.

Although commonly regarded as a concoction of Italian fishermen at Fisherman's Wharf, this sort of dish, like bouillabaisse to the French or *zuppa di pesce* to the Italians, is no stranger to the Dalmatians, many of whom call it *brodetto*.

Serves six to eight.

Basic Recipes

Hollandaise Sauce

5 egg yolks
2 small lemons
Dash of hot sauce
Dash of Worcestershire sauce
1½ cups warm clarified butter

Place a tureen into a pan of previously boiling hot water. Allow tureen to heat for 1 minute. Break egg yolks into tureen. Add strained juice of 1¼ lemons. Do not use bottled lemon juice. Add hot sauce and Worcestershire sauce. Beat or whip vigorously. While continuing to whip, slowly add warm clarified butter. Sauce will thicken. Add more lemon to taste, if desired.

Cream Sauce

2 tablespoons butter
2 tablespoons flour
1 cup cream
Salt and pepper to taste

Heat butter in saucepan. Blend in flour, and cook until bubbly. Add cream gradually, stirring constantly. Cook until thickened. Add salt and pepper. To thicken, use more butter and flour. To thin, use less butter and flour.
Makes 1 cup.

Brown Sauce

2 tablespoons butter
2 tablespoons flour
1 cup beef stock, or instant or cube bouillon
    and water
Salt and pepper to taste

Heat butter in saucepan. Blend in flour. Stir over low heat until flour is brown. Add beef stock gradually, and cook until thickened, stirring constantly. Add salt and pepper.
Makes 1 cup.

Fish Stock

1 tablespoon butter
1 tablespoon chopped onion
1 tablespoon chopped carrot
1 tablespoon chopped turnip
Fish bones, head, tail, and fins
1 stalk of celery
Sprig of parsley
Sprig of thyme
1 bay leaf
1 tomato, or a slice of lemon
1½ quarts water
Salt and pepper to taste

Put butter, onion, carrot, and turnip in a saucepan. Fry them without browning, then add fish bones, head, and trimmings, celery, parsley, thyme, bay leaf, and tomato or lemon slice. Cover with water, and let simmer for an hour or more. Season with salt and pepper. Strain.

Tartar Sauce

    1 cup mayonnaise
1½ tablespoons sweet pickle relish
    1 chopped green onion
    1 teaspoon lemon juice

Combine all ingredients and chill.
Keep refrigerated.

Cocktail Sauce

1¾ cups catsup
    6 tablespoons water
    1 teaspoon white wine
    ¼ teaspoon Worcestershire sauce
    2 or 3 drops of hot sauce

Combine all ingredients and chill.
Keep refrigerated.

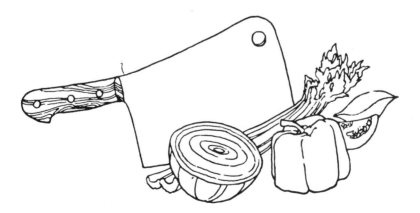

How To Buy a Fish

Fish products, high in protein, are a major source of food in this country. But while there is mandatory inspection of meat and poultry to insure that consumers buy safe and wholesome products, there is no required inspection of fish and fishery products. As a result, you must really be a more selective and informed shopper when selecting seafood. But how?

To help you determine quality when buying fish, the United States Department of Commerce's National Marine Fisheries Service (NMFS) has developed a list of things to look for in determining whether seafood is safe and fresh. This list is the same one used by federal inspectors under a new voluntary fish inspection program, which NMFS is conducting. Under the program, fish processors and canners can pay for federal inspectors to examine their fish and certify that they have been found to be safe, wholesome, and of a good quality.

Fishery products certified under the voluntary inspection program carry on their packages inspection marks indicating quality.

NMFS estimates that about 30 percent of the fishery products processed in the United States are inspected under the new program. These include canned tuna and these frozen items: fried fish, fish cakes, fish dinners, breaded shrimp, scallop products, and seafood platters. However, most fresh fish is not inspected because the consumer can see, touch, and smell it to determine its freshness. But to do this, you need to know what to look for.

Adapted from *Consumer News*, Vol. 5, No. 18, Sept. 15, 1975 (Washington, D.C.: Department of Health, Education, and Welfare).

Selecting Fresh Seafood

Fish

1. First look at the eyes, which should be bright, clear, and protruding slightly from the head. If the eyes have sunken into the head, the fish is probably not fresh.

2. Next check the gills. They should be bright red or pink. As quality slips, the gills begin to darken.

3. If the fish is gutted, turn it over and look at the intestinal cavity, which should be pink and have a fresh, clean appearance.

4. Any fresh cut of fish should have firm flesh, which will spring back when gently pressed with your finger. The skin should be shiny, and the fish should have a mild, clean odor.

In addition to determining the freshness of the fish, you must also decide what form of fish to buy. Fresh fish is usually sold in these forms:

• Whole or round fish. If you select this form, you must scale and gut the fish before you cook it. You will probably be able to use about 60 percent of the fish once it is scaled and gutted and once the head, tail, and fins are removed.

• Dressed. This form of fish is cleaned (scaled with the head, tail, and fins removed) and ready to cook. Since it still has the bones and skin, you will be able to eat about 80 percent of this form.

• Fish steaks. This form consists of cross-section slices of a large, dressed fish. Once you remove the bones, you can use about 90 percent of this form.

• Fillets. This form consists of slices of fish, cut away from the backbone and ready to cook. In this form, you can use 100 percent of the fish.

In deciding which form of fish to buy, NMFS suggests that you consider the cost per edible pound in terms of both convenience and waste. With fish that are bony or hard to prepare, it may pay to buy a form that, although more expensive per pound, has more edible flesh.

Crabs and Lobsters

If crabs or lobsters are fresh, look for movement of the legs. If there is no movement, they are probably dead. Don't buy.

Clams and Oysters

• Clams and oysters should be alive when bought in the shell. If the shells are closed, the shellfish are alive. If the shell is open, tap it gently to see if it closes. If it doesn't, the shellfish is probably dead and should be rejected.
• Check shucked oysters for plumpness and to see if they have a natural creamy color and are in a clear liquid.

Shrimp

Fresh shrimp is sold "green" — raw and in the shell, with or without head.

Frozen Seafood

Fish

• Make sure the fish is solidly frozen and has no objectional odor.

• Frozen fish may be glazed (dipped in water one or more times and quickly frozen to produce an icy glaze that protects the fish from dehydration). As long as the glaze remains intact and the fish remains frozen, it will keep well. If the glaze has melted or is chipped, the unprotected fish may turn a cottony white. This effect is called "freezer burn" and, even though the fish is still frozen, the exposed flesh has begun to suffer a cellular breakdown and should be rejected.

• Avoid damaged packages. Fish is packed in moisture and vaporproof materials to prevent dehydration and contamination. If the package is damaged, it could mean quality loss. Also, don't buy packages stacked above the freezing line in the store freezer. They may be thawed or in the process of thawing.

Shrimp

Frozen shrimp is sold according to color and count size — the smaller the size of the shrimp, the less expensive per pound. Count size per pound should be listed somewhere on the package. The sizes run: 1–5 shrimps, 6–10, 11–15, 16–20, 21–25, 26–30, 31–35, 35 shrimp or more.

Canned Seafood

• Check the condition of the can. If it is bulging, something has broken the seal, and the fish may be spoiled. If the can is dented or rusty, there is no way to know if the seal has been broken.

• When you open the can, check to make sure that the flesh is firm. If the meat is overcooked, the flesh next to the can will be darker. In this case, return the fish to the store.

• If the fish is packed in oil, the oil should be clean, not milky. Also, the can should be properly filled to the top. If it isn't, it should be returned.

• When buying canned tuna, be a label watcher. Albacore is the only kind of tuna that can be labeled "white meat." "Light meat" tuna comes from the yellow fin, skip jack, and blue fin varieties. If the can contains bonita, a fish very much like tuna, it must be labeled "bonita."

Storing Fish

Once you have made your fish selection and have brought the product home, how can you keep it? According to the NMFS you can follow several steps to help retain the quality of fishery products until you use them.

• Store canned products away from heat. When you open them, remove the contents from the can and store in glass or plastic container.

• To freeze fresh fish, divide the fish into small portions and then double wrap it to eliminate air. You can insure a good seal by folding the open end of the wrap several times. Then lay the fish flat in the freezer to freeze it quickly.

How to Prepare Live Crabs and Lobsters

Crabs and lobsters have usually been boiled when you purchase them from the dealer. However, if you buy live fish, drop them into a pot of boiling water and allow them to cook for 20 or 30 minutes, according to size. Add a tablespoon of salt for each gallon of water, and cover the pot.

Crabs and lobsters should be killed by immersion in boiling water. Do not accept uncooked shellfish unless they are alive.

Abalone

The abalone is found along the California coast. The coastal waters shelter green, black, and pink abalone, but it is the red abalone that is of commercial importance.

The abalone is 7 inches or more in its greatest diameter. It has a very strong shell. With the assistance of a large muscular foot, which forms almost the entire contents of its shell, it is able to exert a tremendous pressure by which it holds itself onto the rocks.

Abalone steaks should be well pounded in order to make them tender enough to be palatable. Since the law prohibits the shipping of this shellfish from the state, the people of California may enjoy abalone to the fullest extent.

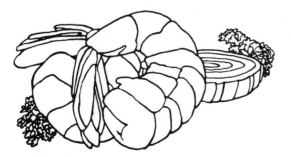

Best Bay Area Seafood Markets

Chinatown offers the best chance for fresh seafood, some of which can be brought home live, swimming in a bucket. (To procure live trout for *truite au bleu,* however, you must contact a fish hatchery, or catch them yourself at Lake Lagunitas in Marin.) Chinatown prices tend to be lower and its varieties most unusual, with live Dungeness and soft-shelled crab, fresh anchovies, abalone, terrapin, and tiny cockles. But you need to be finicky even in Chinese fish stalls.

At Fisherman's Wharf, you'll no longer see fish for the tourists, though it's easy to stop for a live crab or a Maine lobster (from **Fisherman's Seafood Inc.,** Pier 47, 776–6727). Although the dockside warehouses behind Jefferson Street and at the foot of Leavenworth are nominally wholesale, you may find it profitable to scout these places in the mornings for "leftovers."

The city holds many excellent seafood sources, so don't give up when one highly respected purveyor tells you "there are no fresh bay scallops or sea urchins in San Francisco" or "fresh salmon is out of season."

Request special filleting jobs and order even ubiquitous sole in advance. Ask for the trimmings, frames, and heads to use for stock, chowder, and sauce bases. Present the fish eye, as the Chinese do, to a venerated elder. To protect freshness, carry a cooler when you're not going directly home from the fishmongers. Once home, refrigerate your purchase — on ice.

Super Koyama
1790 Sutter
921–6529

The Koyama family runs this wonderfully neat, clean and well-lit market in Japantown. It's worth the visit if only for the variety of hard-to-find Japanese grocery items. Your appetite for sashimi will rise when you see the inviting and abundant displays of beautifully trimmed fish. (They also stock some meats.) Fish selections, which are not limited to sashimi and sushi, depend on seasonal availability. Fresh basics include maguro, hamachi and salmon. Also on hand: cod, pollock roe, sliced cuttle fish, pickled shad roe, mini asahi clams for soup stock, octopus, and herring roe. In addition to traditional sashimi and sushi Super Koyama will clean and cut any fish to order.

Gulfspray
609-611 Cole
751–0473

Just off busy Haight Street exuberant Dale Sims
and partner Eric Matteson sell fresh fish seven
days a week to the public as well as to some of the
Bay Area's finest restaurants from San Francisco
to Sacramento (including Postrio, Cafe Majestic
and the Pacific Heights Bar and Grill). Sims used
to teach school, then started cooking at the Hayes
Street Grill, when he decided to sell fish. "We have
the best white fish around as well as live lobsters
and live crab. We fly in a lot of fish ourselves and
have a large selection with good turnover. We deal
directly with several boats locally and buy only the
best; for example we buy "mooching" salmon, fish
that is caught by fly casting rather than trolling."
Selections also include catfish, cooked crab, golden
trout fillets, ahi tuna, sturgeon, green lip mussels
and oysters.

Canton Market
1100 Grant Avenue
362–5588

Curried crab and light, tender fish balls are among
the deli specialties available almost daily in this
market known, like the nearby Sang Sang, for
having one of the most extensive arrays of
gleamingly fresh fish (much of it moderately
priced) in town. Unlike most fish markets,
however, the Canton smells good, and the floor is
not awash with brine.

Yum Yum Fish
2181 Irving
566-6433

Yum Yum Fish combines the artistic sensibility of
a Japanese owner with the European training of
a French manager. This tidy fish shop next to a
popular neighborhood produce store at 22nd and
Irving has a "sushi deli counter" (they make it to
order for take-out) as well as a traditional market
that features whole fish, fillets, clams, and oysters.
Yum Yum specializes in the freshest local seafood
at good prices from trusted sources in the Gulf of
Mexico, Rhode Island and Hawaii. Says one of their
buyers: "Thanks to the miracle of air freight I can
buy clams from New Zealand cheaper by air than
I can buy clams dug in Washington State. And
because our market is backed by a wholesale fish
company (Nikko Fish) we have variety; it may be
papio from Hawaii, or striped bass from Virginia
or spot prawns from Monterey Bay."

Antonelli's
Cal Mart Super Market
3585 California Street
752-7413

Antonelli's provides yet another good reason to
visit this exceptionally fine supermarket
patronized by Presidio Heights shoppers who
demand high quality and good service and don't
flinch at paying for it. Tony Antonelli, who owned
a Market Street fish emporium before opening this
shop, selects his local fresh fish daily (always lots
of petrale sole, the best-seller) and imports
Mexican prawns and Australian lobster tails.

California Sunshine Fine Foods, Inc.
144 King Street

California Sunshine specializes in caviar, domestic and imported. They produce their own sturgeon caviars (the Tsar Nicolai Mandarin Beluga™ and Mandarin Osetra™) in Russia and northern Manchuria which are featured at such restaurants as Fournou's Ovens and Stars in San Francisco, the Four Seasons in New York and The Mansion at Turtle Creek. In addition to domestic caviar, American Golden Caviar™ from the roe of Great Lakes' whitefish, this company also distributes smoked salmon and fresh and smoked sturgeon.

Excelsior Fish and Poultry
4555 Mission Street
334–6106

Displaced Easterners will be thrilled at the catch in this well-known market, which carries not only the best Pacific Coast seafood but also imports a wide variety from around the country: Florida pompano, Maryland oysters, the basslike croaker, Louisiana buffalo fish and fresh-water catfish, white and large-mouth bass, Speigel carp, Idaho trout, Virginia scallops, and steelhead salmon from Oregon and Washington. It's hard to beat the assortment, including common local fish as well as mahi mahi (which tastes much like swordfish and can be prepared similarly), octopus, and squid. Excelsior's fish and poultry is sold at the outlets listed below, too, but you'll have a greater range of choices if you take the time to visit this Outer Mission District jewel.

PJ's Oyster Bed
737 Irving (Irving near 9th St.)
566-7775

The attractive window display at PJ's Oyster Bed, which lures customers to both the seafood market and restaurant, changes daily to highlight what's in season. The market always has clams and a minimum selection of three kinds of oysters. Recent choices: Hog Island Sweetwaters from Tomales Bay, Totens from Oregon and Little Skookums from Washington State. PJ's also carries over 30 different kinds of fish including an excellent selection from Hawaii (Broad Bill Swordfish, Ahi tuna, Mong Chong, Ono and Parrot fish.) From local sources they get Pacific red snapper, farm-raised Norwegian King Salmon, Idaho trout as well as halibut and petrale sole. Their tanks feature live Maine lobsters and Dungeness crab. And if they don't have the fish you want they'll try to get it for you. Items from the restaurant menu are available for take-out including the chef's crab bisque and unusual chutneys.

Outlets

Clement Farmer's Market at 5th and Clement, 407 Clement, 386-1454
Good Life Grocery, 1524 20th Street, 282-9204
Grand Central Market, 2435 California, 931-4326
Lick Super, 350 7th Avenue, 386-4535

Onorato and Company Louisiana Fish, 1540
Fillmore, 921–1584

Pacific Fish and Poultry, 2414 San Bruno Ave,
468–2355

Plaza Foods, Fulton and Masonic, 567–3855.
United Fish and Poultry.

Seafood Center, 831 Clement, 752–3496

Shirley Fish, 5503 California, 386–1615

Stonestown Fish and Poultry, 255 Winston
Drive, 681–5380

La Rocca's Oyster Bar
3519 California
387–4100

You can buy fresh trout, sand dabs, rex sole,
petrale, prawns, scallops, shad roe, or oysters to
cook at home, or you can order them prepared in
this rather tony setting. Toss in a salad and a
glass of wine and call it lunch. You'll be in good
hands: The owners were trained at Swan's.

Lee Sang Fish Market
1207 Stockton
989–4336

The market sometimes has fresh frogs and
terrapin in addition to a big selection of fish —
which will be cleaned if you request it.

Rossi's
Valley Pride Market
476 Castro Street
431–1128

Known for choice selections and a helpful attitude,
Joe Fisher will take the trouble to debone chicken
at no extra cost, for example, or roll and stuff

petrale with shrimp. Also available: rabbit, fresh herbs, caul fat, and fresh veal sweetbreads. Fisher will also order anything for you, including big freezer offers.

Sang Sang Fish Market
2687 Mission
282–9339

1143 Stockton
433–0403

Part of the fun of shopping at these markets is watching dextrous employees reach into the saltwater bin of wriggling crabs and pull out a live one. At the Chinatown store, the daily specials are printed in Chinese on the wall, but don't worry: Some English is spoken at both stores. If the weather isn't too rough, Sang Sang will have fresh anchovies and is also excellent for fresh abalone, mussels, Blue Point crabs, brine shrimp, fish heads for chowder-making, squid, and Monterey prawns with roe still inside. If it swims in water, Sang Sang probably has it.

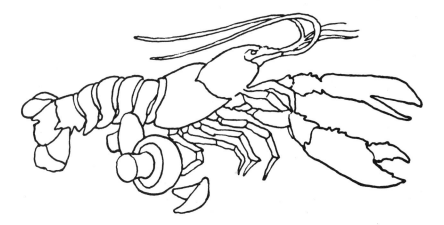

Sunset Super
2425 Irving
759–9110

Reputed to have the best fish in the Sunset District, Sunset Super doesn't sacrifice quantity for quality. In addition to a great deal of knowledge and patience, they offer fillet of petrale sole, rock cod, "red snapper," rex sole, perch, butterfish, sturgeon, English sole, fresh Idaho trout, whole ling cod, ling cod steaks, ling cod fillets, and English kippers, plus crabs, prawns, East Coast scallops, and Pacific Coast Spiny lobsters — sometimes fresh, sometimes frozen — from Baja California. They also will prepare seafood dishes for you to pick up for dinner (petale fillets rolled and stuffed with shrimp, crab thermidor, and others) and share their recipes.

Swan Oyster Depot
1517 Polk Street
673–1101, 673–2757

Sal Sancimino's sons are continuing their father's tradition of dishing out jokes and excellent food from behind their long narrow bar. At Swan's, usually the only store in town for tiny fresh bay scallops and crayfish, the brothers six even make their own caviar for you to take home or eat at the counter with oyster crackers. The finest, liveliest — and costliest — fish depot in town, Swan's is not the place to shop if you have to ask the price. Noted for personal service, Swan's is always packed with loyal devotees who want care, attention, and advice with their fresh, already cracked crab.

Tokyo Fish Market
1908 Fillmore
931–4561

This miniscule family-run operation manages to squeeze produce baskets and a fish counter between its well-filled shelves. When they're not busy, the friendly owners will clean your squid and slice your *sashimi*.

Uoki Sakai
1656 Post Street
921–0515

On Saturdays, this bustling supermarket is busier than Tokyo, for it contains every ingredient necessary for the Japanese kitchen — and then some. What may be the world's largest box of Hershey's kisses is a prize on one of the shelves. Produce is fresh, and the broad sweet Japanese chives beg to be taken home and freely used. The fishmongers are as deft as *sushi* chefs. Hawaii is represented with *poi*, king's bread, and huge buckets of *takuan* (pickled radishes). Prolong your life as you navigate the crowded aisles by purchasing the package of spices to mix with sake for *toso*, the ninth-century Japanese New Year's drink thought to enhance longevity.

East Bay

Berkeley Bowl Seafood, 2777 Shattuck Avenue,
  Berkeley, 548–7008
Monterey Fish, 1582 Hopkins Street, Berkeley,
  525–5600
Monterey Fish in Piedmont, 859 Piedmont
  Avenue, Oakland, 658–9672
Some people think it's worth the trip to the East
Bay to shop at the Monterey Fish Markets. Owner
Paul Johnston only buys fresh fish from local
purveyors all over the US and supplies such
restaurants as Chez Panisse, Bay Wolf and Fourth
Street Grill.
Rockridge Fish Market, Market Hall, 5655
  College Avenue, Oakland, 654–FISH
Spenger's Fish Grotto, 1919 4th Street,
  Berkeley, 845–7771 (Restaurant), 548–2717
  (Fish market)
Sportsmen's Cannery, 67th & Hollis Avenue,
  Emeryville, 655–2282. Sells and smokes
  sportfishermen's salmon.
Ver Brugge, 6321 College Avenue, Oakland,
  658–6854

Marin County

Caruso's, Foot of Harbor Boulevard, Sausalito,
  332–1015
Greenbrae Fish and Poultry, Petrini's, 270 Bon
  Air Shopping Center, Greenbrae, 461-1590
Johnson Oyster Company, Point Reyes,
  669–1149
Paoli Meats, 1 Blackfield Drive, Tiburon,
  383–8522
Tomales Bay Oyster Company, Point Reyes,
  663–1242
Western Boat Shop, 101 Third Street,
  San Rafael, 454–4177
Fresh fish counter (including Dungeness crab in
season) with good selection in a bait and tackle
shop.

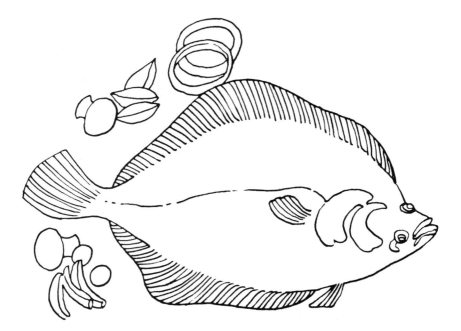

Index of Recipes

NOTES

NOTES

NOTES

NOTES

NOTES

NOTES

NOTES

NOTES

NOTES

NOTES

NOTES